St. Helena Library

St. Helena Public Library
1492 Library Lane
St. Helena, CA 94574
(707) 963-5244

ST. HELENA LIBRARY

J599.74

The Brown Bear

Giant of the Mountains

text by Valérie Tracqui
photos by the BIOS Agency

 Charlesbridge

Library of Congress Cataloging-in-Publication Data
Tracqui, Valérie.
[Ours brun, géant des montagnes. English]
The brown bear: giant of the mountains/text by Valérie Tracqui;
photographs by the BIOS agency.
p.   cm.—(Animal close-ups)
Summary: Examines the physical characteristics, habits, and
habitats of the brown bear.
ISBN 0-88106-439-4 (softcover)
1. Brown bear—Juvenile literature. [1. Brown bear. 2. Bears.]
I. BIOS Agency. II. Title. III. Series.
QL737.C27T7413 1998   96-35947
599.74'46—dc20

Copyright © 1995 by Éditions Milan
300, rue Léon-Joulin, 31101 Toulouse Cedex 100, France
Original edition first published by Éditions Milan under the title *l'ours brun, géant des montagnes*
French series editor, Valérie Tracqui
Translated by Boston Language Institute

Copyright © 1998 by Charlesbridge Publishing
Published by Charlesbridge Publishing, 85 Main Street, Watertown, MA 02172 • (617) 926-0329
All rights reserved, including the right of reproduction in whole or in part in any form.
Printed in Korea
10 9 8 7 6 5 4 3 2 1

The bear has a variety of poses that look almost human. It can stand, squat, sit down, walk upright, and use its front paws like hands.

Patience

In the early summer it is already warm in the mountains. The faint sounds of people drift up from the valley below: a car roars, a dog barks, and children shout.

In the middle of a deep forest, two woodpeckers hammer at the trees. Higher in the mountains, a brown bear lies on a rock above the tree line. As a wild vulture circles in the sky, the bear lumbers into a dense thicket. It is careful to avoid people, and it will wait patiently for night to fall before leaving its hiding place to begin its nocturnal rounds.

Bears live in many different habitats, but they prefer regions with mountain forests, river valleys, and open meadows.

Mountain giant

The brown bear is a giant, and its strength is amazing. It can drag a prey three times its weight, turn over a 200-pound rock, and break a tree trunk with a blow of its paw. Despite its strength, the bear is a peaceful animal and rarely attacks without being provoked.

Like humans, the bear is a plantigrade, a flat-footed animal. It walks on the soles of its feet, not on its toes like the deer or the horse.

The bear has large paws with five claws. The claws on the front paws are especially good for digging up roots and vegetables.

The brown bear's coat varies in color. It can be light brown, tan, or even a dark brown that looks almost black.

Male brown bears are larger and heavier than the females. They are usually between five and eight feet long and weigh between 150 and 800 pounds.

Young brown bears can use their powerful claws to climb trees like cats. When they are fully grown, they stand on their hind legs and shake the tree trunks to make tasty insects fall out.

The bear is very smart and has an excellent memory. It can remember the best places and times of the year to find food. The bear also has strong senses of sight and smell, and at night it uses them to search its territory for prey.

The bear's territory can be between 10 and 130 square miles, and it usually overlaps with the territories of other bears. The bear uses its territory well and can cover up to fifteen miles in one night in search of food.

Sometimes the bear stops for a bath. It loves the water, but it hates to get its ears wet.

Despite its fearsome reputation, the bear does not often prey upon sheep and other livestock.

In the summer, the bear pulls bark off trees with its teeth and claws so it can eat the sweet, tender wood.

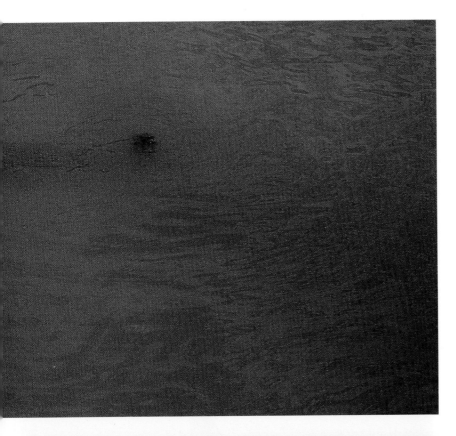

A loner

During most of the year, bears that do not have young cubs travel their territories alone, moving from one area to another to find food. They must eat an enormous amount during the summer and fall to prepare for a long winter of fasting.

The bear will eat almost anything in its territory, both animal and vegetable. People often think of bears as ferocious predators, but they actually kill very few animals for food. They may eat an occasional mouse or squirrel, or a newborn moose or deer, and some lucky bears live near streams full of salmon, but most of their food comes from fruits and vegetables.

Male and female bears mate between May and July. They stay together for several weeks, but when the mating season is over, they go their separate ways.

9

A greedy eater

In the summer the bear feeds on insects, roots, bulbs, mosses, and other vegetation. When fall comes, it looks for ripe fruit. It spends hours carefully using its clawed paws to pick berries. It also rips open anthills to feast on fat worker ants. To gain enough weight to last through the winter, the largest brown bears can eat between eighty and ninety pounds of food a day, gaining three to six pounds of fat.

Suddenly, the bear hears the buzzing of wild bees. The smell of honey gets stronger as the bear hurries toward the hive. Standing upright on its hind paws, it sticks its muzzle in among the bees. The honey tastes so good that the bear ignores the bee stings.

The bear is a hunter and gatherer. It takes advantage of any source of food it can find, and it often will feed on carrion, or dead animals.

More than three-quarters of the bear's food consists of fruits and vegetables. It will eat all parts of them, including the stalks, leaves, and roots. The rest of its diet is made up of insects and mammals.

Before winter

The final weeks of fall, when the first snows come, are very important for the brown bear. This is the last chance for it to eat enough food to get through its long winter fast. In the forest, it gobbles up acorns, looting the stores hidden by other animals.

When it smells something unusual, the brown bear crouches down and stays absolutely still.

In the fall, hunters disturb the bears when they most need peace to feed themselves and prepare for winter.

The bear uses its claws to mark its territory on the trunks of trees.

The bear spends hours digging and scratching the ground for nuts, which are rich in oil. Its body absorbs the fat from the nuts, forming a large, full bump above its shoulders.

During the colder weather of the fall, the egg the female has been carrying since the summer begins to develop. She will give birth to her cubs around six to eight months after mating. Brown bears usually have one to three cubs at a time. The size of each litter depends on the weather conditions and the food supply.

The bear's massive body is protected from the cold by dense fur that grows thicker for the winter.

The bear leaves its giant paw print in the mud.

The bear's den can be in a cave, under a rock, in a hollow tree, or even in a hole. Some bears use the same den year after year.

14

Safe and warm

The pregnant female bear now must choose the place where she is going to spend the winter. Leaving the valleys and meadows, she climbs a steep rocky slope to reach her den. She has already stopped eating, and now she will live off the fat she stored in her body throughout the summer and fall.

She will soon fall into a deep sleep. By resting during the winter months, she saves energy during a season when she would not be able to find enough food to survive. While she rests, her heart and breathing rates slow down, although her body temperature does not drop much. She is able to wake easily, so her sleep is not a true hibernation.

The bear removes stones from its den and uses moss, grass, and small branches as cushions.

15

Birth

One night in January, deep within her den, the bear gives birth to two cubs, a male and a female. Blind and deaf, they look like puppies. They only weigh about one pound each, and they seem small and fragile next to their giant mother. She licks them gently and helps them nurse. For three months, they feed on her rich milk and do not leave the shelter of the den.

As winter ends, the mother goes out more and more often, leaving her offspring behind. She is thin after her long fast and needs to look for food. If she is lucky, she will find the carcass of an animal that did not survive the winter.

As the snow melts, the bear begins to eat and drink again.

Rodents make a good snack for a hungry bear just coming out of its den.

16

After a long winter of fasting, the bear may have lost almost 40 percent of its weight, but its huge head is still impressive.

The cubs will nurse for several more months, but as soon as they leave their den, they start to find other food. Some cubs may gain up to two hundred pounds in their first year.

This growing cub still depends on its mother for protection and security.

By the time they are four or five months old, the cubs are already covered with thick fur as they begin to explore the world around them.

First outing

Finally, around the middle of April, the cubs are allowed to leave the den. They only weigh about five pounds and are very vulnerable. Curious about everything, they love to play, but their mother forbids them to leave her side. She calls them to her by growling, and she will slap or spank them if they disobey. She is strict with them because their survival depends on how well they learn to fend for themselves.

Today she has a treat for the cubs. She leads them to a small pool where frogs have laid thousands of eggs that will make a feast for the young cubs. Imitating their mother, they learn to grab the eggs with fast swipes of their paws.

Growing up

By the time summer arrives, the cubs are eating a lot and growing quickly. While they learn to search for food, their mother scratches her back on the trees. The resin in the tree trunks makes her shed her thick winter coat.

By the fall, the cubs weigh almost fifty pounds and are very agile. They play constantly, chasing each other and tumbling about.

The cubs are becoming more independent, but they will stay with their mother for another year or more. The mother's territory covers about twelve square miles and is part of the larger territory of a male brown bear.

These cubs may look fierce, but they are actually just playing.

The cubs measure their strength in pretend combat.

The eight-month-old cubs are growing stronger, but sometimes they still need their mother's help. An adult male bear suddenly appears at the end of the path. The mother is very protective of her young, and she stands up on her hind legs to watch the intruder. Roaring with anger, she takes a few steps toward him and bares her fangs. The male does not want to start a fight, so he moves away quietly.

Separate ways

Time passes quickly, and the young bears are now two years old. They often wrestle with each other to discover which one is stronger. Their mother is pregnant again, and she gets impatient with her grown children. Finally she chases them from her territory.

The cubs slowly move away. They will roam for a long time, looking for separate territories where they can find food all year long and safe dens in which to spend the winter. The cubs do not meet any other bears along the way, but they must be careful to hide from any people they might see.

Bears continue to search for territories that are remote and undisturbed.

The young bears will face many dangers, but if they are smart and lucky, they may live to be more than twenty-five years old.

Save the bears

Brown bears have always been hunted for their meat, fur, and fat, or just for the thrill of killing such a giant animal. Today this hunting is restricted, but bears face other dangers. Much of their natural habitat has been lost to logging, roads, towns, and housing developments. Now there are organizations all over the world working to save brown bears and their natural homes.

Forest trails and roads, which are carved out by bulldozers, disturb the bears' territories.

A long decline

Brown bears can be found in North America, eastern and western Europe, across northern Asia, and in Japan. There are about 135,000 of them throughout the world, more than any other species of bear. This may sound like a lot, but their population worldwide has actually dropped dramatically. In the 1800s, there were thought to be between 50,000 and 100,000 just in North America.

Counting bears

An important job for conservationists working to save bears is to find out how many bears there are and whether their numbers are growing or shrinking. This can be hard to do, since so many bears live in remote areas. One way to keep track of individual bears is to catch them and put special radio collars on them. Each radio sends off a signal that tells researchers where the bear is, even if it is roaming in a huge territory. Other methods for keeping track of bears include tagging them and counting them from airplanes or on foot.

A road runs through a valley in the territories of several bears. Roads like these deprive bears of their freedom to roam the land.

Refuge

Some of the largest populations of brown bears in North America can be found in southwestern Alaska. Three important sanctuaries have been established to protect these giant bears and their habitat. In the islands that make up the Kodiak National Wildlife Refuge, between 2,500 and 3,000 brown bears now live in an area where they had once almost disappeared. The numbers of brown bears are also increasing in the McNeil River Sanctuary and Katmai National Park. Other efforts to protect and encourage populations of brown bears are taking place all over the world.

A broken territory

There is often a conflict between people who want to save bears and their territory and people who want to hunt bears and use the land. Bears need wide areas of undisturbed wilderness, but the amount of natural habitat available is shrinking rapidly. Even in remote mountains, roads are cut through so the forests can be used by people. Bears are often disturbed by hikers, campers, and mountain bikers.

Due to the work of environmentalists, this young bear has a much better chance of surviving to adulthood.

The bear family

The brown bear is one of the eight species of the Ursidae family. All of these species are powerful hunters with large clawed paws. Their food varies depending on the season, from small fruit to larger prey like rodents, fish, or even livestock. Most of them take long winter rests but do not truly hibernate.

▲ The *American black bear* lives in the forests of Canada and the United States. Often it climbs trees to steal birds' eggs or bees' honey. These bears, which range in color from very dark to almost blond, are considered threatened in some parts of the United States.

◄ The *Himalayan black bear,* or *moon bear,* is found mostly in the forests along the Himalaya Mountains in south-central Asia. This small bear moves mostly at night, but it can be recognized in the darkness by the white crescent on its chest. Its hearing and sight are very weak, but its strong sense of smell lets it know where it is going and helps it find food.

The *polar bear* is the largest land carnivore in the world. Some males weigh more than 1,300 pounds and are more than eleven feet tall when they stand upright. Living on the coasts of the North Pole, this giant bear is well adapted to ice and cold. Its large paws, covered with fur, let it move without sliding on the ground. Its fur and a thick layer of fat protect it from cold and allow it to swim for hours in icy water. The polar bear loves to hunt seals and fish.

▶

◀ The *grizzly bear* is an American subspecies of the brown bear. Once common throughout North America, it is now only found in larger numbers in Alaska and Canada. It has been protected in the lower forty-eight states since 1975, when it was placed on the Endangered Species list. At present, there are about thirty thousand grizzlies in North America, but only one thousand in the continental United States.

Photograph Credits

BIOS Agency:
F. Marquez: covers, p. 6 (right), p. 7 (top), p. 12 (top), p. 13 (left), pp. 18-19, p. 25 (bottom); G. Lopez: pp. 4-5 (full page), p. 8 (bottom left), p. 11 (bottom left and right), pp. 14-15 (full page), p. 14 (bottom left and right), pp. 22-23 (full page), p. 25 (top); Klein-Hubert: pp. 8-9 (top), p. 8 (bottom right), p. 13 (top right), p. 21 (bottom), p. 24 (bottom); P. Henry: p. 3, p. 7 (bottom), pp. 10-11 (full page), p. 21 (top), p. 23 (bottom); Y. Noto Campanella: p. 4 (bottom); J. Y. Grospas: p. 6 (bottom left); C. Ruoso: p. 9 (bottom); J. Mayet: p. 11 (top right); D. Bringard: p. 11 (middle); H. Chelle: p. 12 (bottom); A. Beignet: p. 15 (bottom), p. 20 (bottom); F. Pierrel: p. 16 (top), p. 20 (top); E. Barbelette: p 16 (bottom); L. Nitsch: p. 17; R. Valarcher: p. 26 (bottom); Dani-Jeske: p. 26 (top); F. Bruemmer: p. 27 (top); M. Gilles: p. 27 (bottom)

With thanks to Roland Guichard of the ARTHUS Association and Frédérick Lisak for their collaboration.